Bruised Knuckles and Other Lessons in Faith

Reflections on Reality from a Mentor's Heart

Grant McDowell

WestBow
PRESS
A DIVISION OF THOMAS NELSON

WestBow Press books may be ordered through booksellers or by contacting:

WestBow Press
A Division of Thomas Nelson
1663 Liberty Drive
Bloomington, IN 47403
www.westbowpress.com
1-(866) 928-1240

ISBN: 978-1-4497-2726-0 (sc)
ISBN: 978-1-4497-2725-3 (e)

Library of Congress Control Number: 2011917378

Printed in the United States of America

WestBow Press rev. date: 10/13/2011

To Jim and Mildred McDowell—for showing
me more than telling me how to live

CONTENTS

PREFACE

This collection of thirty-one reflections consists of lessons drawn from life and leadership. One cannot commit inner thoughts to paper without sensing the severe limits of his experience, and so I do not present these reflections as a compendium of wisdom. Rather, these reflections aim to stimulate thought, courage, comfort, faith, and a little humor. Many people deserve thanks for mentoring me through five decades and beyond. I stand on their shoulders, and in many cases, still walk beside them.

INTRODUCTION

These life lessons are intended for individual reflection or dialogue between family members or a small group of friends. Because mentoring has been and continues to be a force shaping my life, this book is offered as a way of awakening conversations with God and ourselves about matters we take too little time to think about. Also, my desire in putting these thoughts on paper is to rekindle conversation between friends and with loved ones about things we need to talk about. Today in North America, a creeping elitism suggests we dare not speak out about the things most precious to us—the matters of the heart. However, without transparency, we have no meaningful relationships with God, ourselves, or each other. Therefore, this book invites reflection and dialogue about simple issues that together weave complex outcomes on the loom of life. Whether you read these alone in an airport, at home, by a bubbling stream in the mountains, or on your patio, my hope is that you will take time to look inside, argue with me, reach out to someone else, and find encouragement. Because this collection consists of thirty-one life lessons, you might read one a day for a month, and then give the book to a friend.

Managing Emotions

────────── ❧ ──────────

Anger

Disillusionment and Discouragement

Stress

1

Anger

Hour after hour crawled across the face of the illuminated clock while I tossed and fumed over a workplace problem I could not solve. Finally, I gave in to the fear looming in the fog of my late-night brain and smashed my fist against the wall. Unfortunately, the wall had been there much longer than I; the cement-like lath and plaster was aged to seventy-year perfection, and the impact rounded my previously pointed knuckles. As a result, the pain distracted me from my anger, at least momentarily.

I was exasperated over my inability to rescue a friend from dangerous choices. I had taken responsibility for his problems. Since both my wife and I were wide awake after the merging of fist and plaster, we talked about the feelings I had bottled and corked. Had I identified and talked about them earlier, I could have saved my knuckles! Though I had done things in the wrong order, hitting the wall not only reshaped my hand, it helped shape my response to anger.

My frustration arose from a sense of powerlessness. In fact, anger often peaks because we have little power to change circumstances or the wills of others. This is a lesson familiar to parents. The will of a child or teenager is not something Mom or Dad controls much of the time. Parents shape, guide, and discipline their children's wills. But they must put appropriate controls in place without crushing the child's will or alienating his or her heart.

Unfortunately, plaster-cracking anger can be addictive. By this I mean it can yield a rush of adrenaline that makes one feel powerful. This false sense of power undermines relationships because it nurtures fear instead of trust. Furthermore, false power deceives one into believing he need not explore the feelings boiling inside. Explosive anger is a shield that hides weakness instead of a real solution to frustration, pain, or powerlessness. Here are some knuckle-saving suggestions for dealing with powerlessness in a better way:

- Admit your pattern is difficult to change and will require hard work.
- Ask yourself what you fear. Anger often disguises fear or hurt.
- Step away from the situation and cool down.
- Be brave enough to lay down your anger. You might be using anger as a shield to keep God, yourself, or others at a distance.
- Admit you cannot handle the problem without God's help.
- Ask God for wisdom to understand and for power to change.

- Recognize and reject the rush that comes from aggression.
- Talk about your frustration instead of bottling it up until it explodes.
- Express your feelings honestly and constructively in a journal.
- Participate in wholesome activities, such as a sport, where you enjoy doing your best and where you feel a measure of legitimate control.
- Get close enough to one mature friend or mentor with whom you can talk about your anger.

Maybe we believe we should be able to expel anger and be done with it. Yet, although exceptions may exist, most of us must manage anger well because we cannot merely drive it out. My plaster lesson is over thirty years old, but I am still learning. As if on cue, my computer froze as I wrote this. No reason. Just a computer gremlin testing the validity of what I am saying. One cannot avoid frustrating situations, but one can learn new coping skills. For example, now is the time for me to walk away from this keyboard; after all, it's not made of plaster.

Reflection: When you feel like exploding in anger, is it most often due to frustration, fear, or something else?

Disillusionment and Discouragement

In my early teens, when a bigger kid threatened to beat me up, one of my friends stood back and said to my assailant, "Kill 'im." The school bus driver stepped in, preventing my untimely death, but I learned a lesson that day: Sometimes people are unreliable when we need them most. In other words, human nature looks out for number one. Those who have not learned this lesson feel disillusioned and afraid to invest their time and emotions in people. When one feels betrayed by a friend, one's battered illusions can leave him or her bitter, angry, or afraid to care for others.

For example, have you ever lived in the illusion that everyone should like you? Have time and experience shattered some of your ideals? Could one or more of the following examples come from your diary?

- "Love for my spouse will always feel romantic."
- "My boss will always be pleasant and affirm my skills."
- "The system will always treat me fairly."
- "My friends will never let me down."
- "If I trust God, life will be easy."

If one believes an illusion, one ends up disillusioned with God, faith, family, church, school, work, and life itself. In other words, illusions rob people of security because illusions inevitably crumble.

One wonders if the illusion of a perfect world is a distant memory of God's perfect creation. Since he created a perfect world, free from pain, hurt, and disillusionment, could illusions be imprints of his perfect design, lingering in the subconscious? Leave that in the *Questions for Heaven* file.

Some of my illusions became targets for reality around the time I entered first grade. I remember the day my mother drove me to school over the hills of our old country lane, giving last minute instructions about how I should behave. I was fresh-faced, looking forward to meeting a bigger world, and I was full of childish naïveté. Nevertheless, school introduced me to a bigger reality. For one thing, I learned that friends did not feel the same way toward me every day, nor did I feel the same way toward them. Moreover, my school experience helped me understand that I was not the center of the world, and neither were my friends. They changed; so did I.

The point is that disillusionment infects everyone who lives in the illusion that life is supposed to be easy. Similarly, discouragement is the result of drawing courage from a finite source. In other words, when one has confidence in an unstable footing, like a friend's personality, one is headed for disappointment. Furthermore, those who base courage on their own ability to overcome every trouble will fail when they can no longer sustain themselves.

Jesus illustrated this when he described the house of a man who built on sand instead of rock. Every building is strong in mild weather, but the sandy foundation was treacherous when a storm struck. By contrast, Jesus said that another house, built on rock foundation, stood firm (Matthew 7:24-27). The point is that one's foundation results in either confidence or fear. When one can say, "I don't get discouraged" because his courage is not built upon shakable sources, and "I don't get disillusioned" because he does not live in illusions, he has taken a giant step toward maturity. The critical lesson is to learn dependence upon God's character, love, and faithfulness rather than the shifting sands of human nature.

Reflection: Have you built your confidence on an illusion? What's your next step to breaking free of this illusion?

Stress

Most of my stress is self-induced. This hit me like a nine iron around the seventh hole where a foursome met one beautiful Saturday. After a couple of ugly swings, I was not having fun. I judged my value by the quality of my play. I became more stressed; my swing became less natural; I became more stressed . . . You get the picture.

Stress climbs high like an undercut golf ball when we try to be in control of everything. And like a poorly hit ball, stress cannot take us the distance. Too much stress results from believing life is all about us, from preoccupation with performance rather than glorifying God. Jesus valued glory over performance when he drew his friends' attention to wildflowers in the field. They were not straining, but they were beautiful. He pointed to sparrows that were not worried about the next season, although they diligently gathered food (Matthew 6:25-33). Often, life-crushing stress arises from a belief that *we* are at the center of the universe.

I have noticed another interesting fact about stress. It is usually a choice. If we buy something we cannot afford, thereby deepening our indebtedness, we experience stressful money problems. In the ensuing months, when bills choke our freedom, we might remember that we chose struggle over simplicity.

The words we speak are also stress factors. Are we willing to live with the results of what we feel like saying in the heat of an angry moment? The Bible compares the tongue to a fire ignited by hell (James 3:6). Once we light the fire, we get burned. How can we manage stress effectively?

Next time we are golfing, going to school, working, or driving and feeling stressed out, we might first ask, "Why are we doing this to ourselves?" Life is not always as simple as we would like, yet we usually have the option to slow down and enjoy good moments. One might also ask, "Will my life be more enjoyable if I just try harder when plans don't turn out as I'd hoped? Are people I care about going to benefit if I devote more energy to achieving success?"

Second, ask, "What is the goal in this situation?" If we do not have a defined goal larger than the current crisis, we ought to figure out what we are aiming for. Once we know the goal, we can begin bringing irritations under control. Goals depend neither on perfection nor performance. For example, as parents, we should make it our goal to be good parents rather than to raise perfect kids. Children and teenagers have wills of their own, and sometimes they make inappropriate decisions just as adults do. Parents feel less stress when they understand choices to be part of life's curriculum.

Third, ask for help. Someone might have resources we need in order to solve a problem, build a deck, or fix a leaky roof. No one is self-reliant. We perfectionists stress ourselves because we expect to do everything well, without depending on others for help. For some of us, asking for help symbolizes failure. We need to get over ourselves! We will be more emotionally healthy when we ask for help, and we will build better friendships. God did not give talents to hoard, but to share. Remember, stress is often a result of our choices.

Reflection: What is a significant stressor in your life right now, and which principle can you apply in order to manage it better?

Nurturing Faith

Church

God

Prayer

Church

I quit going to church, and you should too, if you already have not. "Well," you're thinking, "that's awkward; he's a pastor, and he doesn't go to church. Is this a new Internet fellowship, a blog church, or what?" No, I just quit going to church. Still awkward, since the church pays me to, among other things, teach, counsel, lead, be available, encourage, and sometimes, deal with conflict. But as much as I love the church, I had to quit going to church. "Ha!" you're thinking, "I'd go if they paid me!"

I did not quit because I dislike the *place*; after all, the church is not a place or a building, so for goodness sake, let's stop calling church-owned facilities "The House of the Lord" or "God's House." Sure, you should respect the place, but the Lord has never been keen on being restricted to buildings. He was born in an open, drafty stable, and as the Creator of the universe, he does not need real estate. Sure church buildings are sacred, but so is my car; I have dedicated both to the Lord to be used for his glory, but he is confined neither to the trunk of my car nor to church buildings.

Those of us who know and follow Jesus Christ *are* the church, and frankly, we are a rag-tag bunch when you really get to know us. This is why rich people and famous, popular people do not often like to identify with the church. They have a lot to lose, hanging out with needy people like us. Money and power get people what they want for a while, so wealth and popularity convince people they do not need divine help.

So if the church is not a building but people, why quit going to church? I quit going to church because I have been hurt too much by the people in church. Sorry if you have too because I am part of the church problem, and maybe I have hurt you. But here is the point: if you merely *go* to church, the people there will really, really bug you after while. They are completely human, and nothing is more irritating that a human or a big group of humans, especially when they are trying hard to do the right thing. God knows they can be dangerous; a group of religious people murdered his Son. And if they killed Jesus, imagine what they might do to you!

So, here is my advice: Stop going to church; instead, *become* the church. If you merely attend church, the flaws of those other humans will annoy you to the point that your faith will cool off and you will not care about people anymore. Moreover, if you go to church instead of becoming the church, you will avoid using your gifts and skills to bless others.

On the other hand, if you become the church, you will learn to forgive people as Jesus forgives you. You will realize you are both the problem and the solution to your relationships. And, God will gradually make you more like Jesus. Jesus lives through transparent people. He wants them to be with him so much that he came to earth and took all the pain his torturers could deal. He did that to be everybody's substitute by his death on the cross; then he stepped into hell to set the Devil straight about who's the boss. After that, he rose again from the dead because death could not hold him back.

Do not reject Christ just because church subculture represents him poorly. We who form the church are a dim reflection of Christ. However, we love him, and we are learning to trust him in everyday life. But churches sometimes add extra frills, rules, and unnecessary, even ungodly, traditions to the truth of the New Testament. The Catholics have their no-marriage rule for priests. Evangelicals have, in recent decades, replaced the good news with good marketing. Charismatics sometimes appear to make things up as they go along. And some liberal Protestants are not even sure if Jesus is God's Son.

But if you let other people stand between you and God, you do not have much character. Do not let caricatures of Christ keep you from the real thing. Every church is made up of people, and people mess up. So, please forgive us our sins; we are learning, and we are growing. Well, some of us are not; some of us think we are better than anyone else, but we will find out soon enough that we are dead wrong. And it will not be pretty when God shows us what we are really like. However, you will have to look in his mirror too, so look past the subculture of the church and trust in Jesus Christ. Stop blaming the church for your decisions, and stop going to church. *Be* the church through personal faith in Jesus Christ, and you will find most of the people at church quite lovable. And if you become the church through trusting in Jesus Christ, you will need to be with the rest of the church. That's just how life goes.

Reflection: What can you do to *be* the church *you* would like to join?

God

First, if God is really God and not some projection of our imaginations, might he likely know more than we do? By accepting the rule of God over the universe, we make a life-altering choice to accept his authority and complete knowledge. If we reject God because we cannot understand how both good and evil coexist in the world, we have chosen to be our own gods. If we accept him and the claims of the Bible that he knows all and rules all, we admit that we do not know everything, including the purpose behind events or circumstances that seem beyond redemption.

Certainly, the death of Jesus Christ on the cross looked to his immediate followers like the triumph of evil. Yet a few days later, Christ's followers and more than five hundred others saw him alive and well as he ate with them and taught them before going to heaven. God knew what was to happen. In his redemptive power, no tragedy is without hope and meaning, though to us it appears not to make any sense. Rejecting God on the grounds that we do not understand what's going on betrays our belief that we are at the center of the universe and God is on the perimeter.

Second, those who reject God because of the apparent domination of evil or suffering seldom if ever want God to control their lives as completely as they wish he would control the perpetrators of evil. In fact, refusal to submit to God as the all-knowing ruler of the universe does not guarantee someone else will similarly submit to him. It is contradictory to say, "I can't believe in a God who would allow suffering," when our assumption is that we should be free to choose our own paths. Others are also free to choose and face the consequences of God's justice or accept the power of his mercy. We cannot have it both ways; we cannot legitimately believe in absolute self-determination for ourselves while questioning God's justice for letting tyrants choose to oppress others. God did not ignore the problem of evil but faced it in person through Jesus Christ's death on the cross. The just suffered for the unjust, condemning the grip of evil on the human soul. Jesus endured the judgment of God against evil and rose again to offer life to those who embrace Christ as the Son of God.

Reflection: How much control over your life do you really want God to have?

Prayer

Sometimes answers to prayer do not look like we expect them to. For example, a teenager might blurt out hateful, angry words to his parents, leaving them stunned and hurt. Yet, they had been asking God for a breakthrough in their relationship and now the teenager's gut-wrenching honesty has opened a door into his true feelings.

God might not remove the obstacles blocking the path to our dreams, but he does want to change and empower us to move *through* those obstacles. In fact, the obstacles might be there in order that we become more like the persons God designed us to become. For example, Jesus asked his heavenly Father to remove the cross from his future, if his Father so willed. Then, Jesus declared himself willing to do whatever his Father wanted. Jesus went to the cross; God did not remove it from his path. Instead, Jesus died as the only fitting substitute for us. Had God answered his prayer by taking away the cross, he would have removed this beautiful act of grace—the death and resurrection of Christ. He would have denied us this gateway to his presence.

On the other hand, prayer is the gateway to God's miracles. One of my earliest memories of prayer involves my mother pacing the hallway, praying for me as I shrieked through another vicious headache. When I was a child, my headaches felt like my forehead was lifting off my face. In fact, I imagined I would feel better if it did. I remember when, in answer to Mom's prayer, the pain broke suddenly and the headaches never returned with the same intensity. God hears prayer. I have seen others, suffering from illness and pain, relieved in answer to prayer. At other times, I have prayed for people who are stressed, distressed, oppressed, lonely, or devastated, and God has comforted, encouraged, and renewed them.

I wish I could say I always feel like praying and that prayer is always easy. Sometimes God appears not to answer. Other times, in response to persevering prayer, he steps in and makes a difference. At times, he answers in an instant, and at other times, he answers before I ask. In other words, he does not always answer in the same way.

What I can say after years of praying is that prayer is primarily about God. It is not about getting everything we want. God does not have to answer prayer the way we believe he should in order to defend his reputation. He is not campaigning for our votes. Instead, he is the all-knowing, all-powerful, loving heavenly Father who understands us. Human parents are imperfect, and do not always make right decisions. God, on the other hand, is the perfect Father who sees the big picture. Here are some different kinds of prayer, each focused on God himself:

- The prayer my mother said long ago was intercessory prayer, or prayer that pleads for someone else. Jesus gave an example, teaching us to pray and not give up. He told of a man who went to a friend's house at midnight, asking for bread to feed unexpected company. When he asked his friend for bread, the friend told him to go away since he and his family were already in bed. Finally, Jesus said, because he persisted to ask boldly, and not for the sake of the friendship, the man will give his friend all he needs. By contrast, Jesus said that God *loves to give* to his children, so we ask, believing we will receive (Luke 11:5-9).

- At other times, prayer involves listening more than asking. The Gospels tell us Jesus got up very early to pray. He listened for guidance from his Father. He made it clear that everything he did was the will of God. One day with his disciples, he used the example of a vine and its branches to show how dependent we are on him (John 15). As life and nutrients flow from vine to branch, so spiritual life and power flow from Christ to us. We are the receivers, the listeners, the responders.

- Sometimes confession is our most important theme in prayer. In the Psalms, David confessed his need of forgiveness. After a series of terrible decisions, which made him an adulterer and murderer, he was broken by guilt. But he found forgiveness and new direction when he openly admitted his sin to God (Psalm 51).

- Pray throughout the day. When I am planning a program, preparing a lesson, or helping someone solve a problem, I send up "arrow prayers"—silent pleas for help.
- I have also found it necessary to have a particular time and pattern of prayer. For me, that time is early morning when I follow the pattern Jesus taught his disciples. The Lord's Prayer, as we've come to call it, provides an outline. That way, when I am distracted, I have a pattern to guide me back to prayer. I think of the pattern as an acronym of the word WANT, which stands for Worship, Ask, Not guilty, and Temptation-safe:
  o *W*orship God for his Fatherly love, his perfect holiness, and his absolute authority as King of Kings.
  o *A*sk for the daily things necessary in our material world.
  o *N*ot guilty. His forgiveness is available to those who are repentant and believing.
  o *T*emptation-safe. Christ defeated evil's power when he died on the cross for our sins and rose again. In prayer, we ask for deliverance from evil and protection from temptation.

Prayer is an ongoing conversation between God and us. Do not neglect the powerful truth that God wants you to ask and receive, seek and find, and knock until he opens the door for you. The Father wants to hear *from* you. When children leave home, hearing from them and being available to meet their needs is a parent's delight. How much more would a perfect Father want to hear from us in any circumstance? God answers prayer.

Reflection: What would you like to do today to make prayer a larger part of your life?

Seizing Hope

Quality of Life

Time

Today

Work

Quality of Life

My mother suffered through the lonely, frightening wilderness of Alzheimer's Disease for twelve years before she died. Some said she had no quality of life through many of those years, but I observed quality of life in the unwavering, faithful love my father showed her. And I saw quality of life in the compassion and care she received from the staff at the nursing home.

We often do not understand the true nature of persons. Therefore, we think quality of life depends upon healthy, functional bodies; the old, the sick, and unborn are disposable because we tell ourselves they are not doing what persons do. But persons are spiritual as well as physical. Moreover, the human spirit is unique, created in the image of God who made us like himself.

Although God is Spirit and has no body, he made us with physical bodies that express his likeness in the best way possible in a physical world. And yet, as wonderful as the human body is, we are much more than bodies. We are also created spirits. Our spirits are not confined to our bodies though they are inseparable from them while our bodies have breath. Body and spirit are one until at death our bodies no longer hold our spirits.

So, the spirit does not age, but it needs an awakening so that, in both body and spirit, we can become all we were created to be. This awakening is literally a new birth when God's Spirit reunites with one's human spirit and opens up new dimensions of life. God created persons in his image. He also called us to himself, and a call is no mere invitation but a command. Jesus told his disciples that they must be born again. This is not the rallying cry of a particular kind of church but the words of Jesus himself, a way of saying we need real change that only he can initiate. So his calling is a command, and faith in him is one's first act of obedience.

When we are awakened spiritually, we become aware that we are with God, not estranged from him. This is not merely a matter of becoming spiritual; we were spiritual from birth. Rather, new birth is a new awakening—a moment when God's Spirit breathes new life into our spirits and we change. Nor is this merely a matter of "getting religion." On the contrary, focus on religious ceremony can coat us with a layer of self-righteous epoxy that inhibits us from opening our spirits to God.

In contrast, the awakened spirit grows in closeness, or communion, with God's Spirit. The awakened human spirit is no longer alone in the deepest sense but now has a profound and eternal friendship with God. How can we describe life in the Spirit? Though our physical senses do not often fully experience the Holy Spirit's presence, he is always near. Sometimes, however, we do feel his nearness, and this awareness is like walking with a best friend, yet someone closer than a human friend can be. Being with God's Spirit is like intertwined fingers, except there is no flesh to prevent the union of the spirits. It is, in fact, being in his possession and he in ours. It is the ultimate experience of spiritual and emotional health.

The Spirit of God did not abandon my mother's spirit even when her body, including her brain, was broken. Neither will he abandon any of us when we face the threat of a reduced quality of life.

Reflection: Whom has your mind already discarded as someone with no quality of life?

Time

I waved good-bye to my little boy the other day as he stepped into the school bus and disappeared into the wonderful maze of first grade. Days later, it seems, we shook hands at his high school graduation. Time evaporates before my eyes. This moment is gone, a morsel of eternity. If I dwell on the mystery of time for long, I feel my helplessness and fear insignificance. Time is a mystery that can swallow those who stare into its chasm.

All we know of time is past tense since we cannot see tomorrow and the present evaporates just before we grasp its depth. All that we know of the future, we know by faith. Looking back, time seems compressed, while the future looks barely visible. Only a short time ago, I was a child and then a young person for whom time stretched on like a horizonless road.

When I study my back trail, I realize it's never too soon to begin something. For example, I remember beginning work on a masters degree. I gave little thought to the program's end; it was years in the future. In fact, I squeezed that three-year degree into thirteen! Had I focused on the horizon, I might never have begun. But hindsight compresses time, and the years I spent earning credits and learning lessons now seem like a few fading photos. One can never begin too soon, or too late, to change. Failure might convince us we are tethered to an inescapable past, but to initiate change is to remove the leash of habit from our necks.

Past experience can shape our patterns, including financial habits. Growing up without money made me extra frugal. So when my wife and I saw an antique dining room suite she liked, my first reaction was to point out the price tag. Since we visited the antique store regularly, we checked several times to see if the walnut table and chairs were still there, but seeing the price unchanged, we resigned ourselves to the fact we were not going to own it. On my day off, weeks later, I stopped in to browse, and as usual, stopped to look at the dining room suite. I felt prompted to make an offer I knew would be a stretch to afford, but asked myself, "How many times do I come across something that just seems to be the right one?" I told the clerk that I knew it was a long shot, but she wrote down my offer and said she would call when she had an answer. To my surprise, she called the next day, saying my offer had been accepted. The suite now graces our dining room, and though it stretched our finances at that time, we kept other priorities intact, while enjoying the "new" furniture. Opportunities we have seized in the past are always worthwhile in the present.

While the past can reveal our need to change, the present can teach us to slow down, to squeeze the best juice out of each day. Slowing the pace allows us to do a few things well rather than dozens of things poorly. Anxiety over what we are unable to do never improves the present. We easily overestimate how much we can accomplish in one year, but underestimate how much we could accomplish over a longer time span. So, slow down enough to envision the years to come. Each day is a piece of eternity to embrace and enjoy while keeping the big picture in view. To be healthy, we need little vacation islands in time—minutes, hours, or days when we let the over-burdened boats full of tasks sail by as we rest and resist the temptation to climb aboard every cause. We are human beings not merely "human doings" always striving to get the next responsibility checked off the to-do list. We need time to consciously step into God's embrace and enjoy him or we become frenzied, the present will slip by, and we miss today's unique flavor.

While the past taught us that it is never too soon to begin, and the present is teaching us to slow down, the future teaches us to dream and set higher goals. Life's hurts have a way of taunting dreams and mocking hopes, but we influence the future through dreaming God's dreams for us and setting goals. If parents can dream of their children's success, our Father in heaven must dream of our growing maturity, kindness, and skill, which not only bring him glory but also fulfill our purpose. God gives dreams; in fact, he dreams through us. We may adjust our dreams without throwing them away. Submit them to the Father's leadership and keep dreaming . . . one day at a time. For, even in tiny increments, goals move us toward the fulfillment of our dreams.

Reflection: Think of two or three lessons you have learned from time.

Today

Regret the past, fear the future, or grab hold of today and squeeze the life out of it! Too many people are waiting for the best day to come along—waiting for life to be good to them, to happen *to them!* And too many people are living on yesterday, when their imaginations tell them that life was wonderful. I am not advocating that you paste on a big, stupid grin and pretend today is perfect; people who fake happiness are obnoxious. But I am declaring that this day is the only day God has given you, and you can pine away for yesterday, or put all your hopes in tomorrow if you like. But you will miss today. Many people choose to miss today . . . every day! But even the hard things of today come along for a reason—to teach you something you do not yet know, to show you who you are and, more importantly, to show you who God is.

You can choose to live in the regret, pain, and rejection of the past or the fear of tomorrow, or you may choose to live in today by consciously serving God and people with everything you have. God sees, and he is faithful, even if others pay no attention or show no appreciation.

Today is the best day of your life. You do not have tomorrow. All the resources you gained yesterday and all the dreams of your tomorrows funnel into this one day. So, treasure today as the essence of eternity now—the day you will be all that God has created, called, and gifted you to be. Do not anxiously await a better day though there might be better days. Treat this as your best day—the day you have to give your best work, take your best rest, give your best love—even best grieve your losses—learning all that you can from them.

The best thing in life is knowing God and realizing that he has a purpose in your life. In the midst of all the unanswerable questions, you can have this assurance: peace with God through faith in Jesus. I believe he is alive today and that he gives life certainty and meaning. And today is the day you have to live at peace with God—to give your all at work, no matter now menial the task feels, to dream, to treat others as you would like to be treated, to discover more about your purpose.

The world longs for the new, and so it tries to create substitutes for faith in the living God: more new stuff, more new ways to be happy, more positive thoughts or insights from some imaginary source in the universe. But none of these things last. God alone gives new life. Unfortunately, even followers of Jesus sometimes live as though he is dead. They would rather not embrace today with faith; often, they would rather grieve yesterday.

Today is the best day of your life. Truly, today is the only day you have. Yesterday is over; tomorrow is not guaranteed;

today is what you have. Nothing and nobody can steal this day from you.

Reflection: Would you dare believe that today is the best day of your life? Why or why not?

Work

How do we find satisfaction in work? I was watching construction workers near my home, and I found myself wishing that I had their job. They can see what their hands accomplish each day. By contrast, the results of my work are hard to measure. I invest hours mentoring, caring, coaching, counseling, teaching, praying, leading, and sometimes arguing, but I usually do not go home at night feeling that I have built something. On the contrary, sometimes I leave a day's work feeling drained and overwhelmed because needs and opportunities gather more quickly than I can address them. And I am not alone in this experience. Even those of us who like our work sometimes wonder if it contributes something of lasting value.

However, I wonder if the construction workers take time to step back from *their* work and enjoy it. And I wonder why *I* do not take moments to reflect on what I have accomplished and to give thanks for my work. The nature of work is that it is never complete. I finish a sermon and another sermon is soon due, and those to whom I preach rightly expect me to have something to say! Similarly, the man who frames the house next door completes his task, and then he must move on to another one. His work is covered in exterior finish and his contribution forgotten.

But we ought to take a little time to savor our work. God did this on the seventh day, after he finished creating. He looked at all he had made and saw that it was very good. Then he rested. Why do we neglect moments to savor what we have made? Why not give thanks to God because we have this work to do? Maybe we pointed someone down a path of hope when she was living in fear, or we helped a man learn to let go of a painful past. We built a wall or a roof that will protect a family against extreme cold. We need, like Solomon, to understand the importance of savoring our work (Ecclesiastes 5:18-20).

But does this mean we must always love our jobs? Being grateful for work does not suggest it satisfies our deepest desires and needs. I don't love my work any more, but I like it. I used to love it too much. I was the job; I derived my identity from my work. Then, when it went badly, I was frustrated, angry, or depressed. Now I love Jesus, my wife, my children, and people, and I *like* my work. Work never loves us back; work does not give ultimate satisfaction.

In fact, work can be impersonal. Some jobs are dehumanizing. Some managers treat workers like numbers;, and some work is dead-end and low-paying. More money, however, does not equal job satisfaction. Some highly paid workers strike when they do not get an expected raise or contract. Some professional athletes sit out part of a season demanding *more* millions.

This illustrates, at least in part, why some people with low-paying jobs, like clerks and waitresses, are friendly and accommodating, while some with higher incomes and job security are difficult to deal with. If we measure our worth by wages or benefits, we become greedy. When others make more money, we believe they are more valued. Workers should be well paid, but as long as we interpret our value by our pay scale, we will be dissatisfied. Human dignity is based not on our roles or the size of our paychecks, but on God's love for people.

Of course, the boss might not believe this. Some bosses are unfair. Fearful of losing power, they squelch creativity; they kill new ideas. On the other hand, bosses want a little respect, like people in general, and chances are if we give respect, we receive it. Underneath their roles, bosses are ordinary people with the same challenges others have.

Working my way through college, I had a job one summer as a utility man in a lumber mill. This impressive title meant I was available for whatever needed doing, as long as it did not require experience or skill. My first chore was stacking sticks. Pretty exciting! When the lumber came from the kiln on its way to the planer, lengths of lath tumbled onto a conveyor belt. These strips of lath had separated the rows of boards so that air would circulate around them as they dried. My not-so-rewarding task was sorting the sticks, preserving reusable ones in a stack, and discarding broken ones in a barrel. It was the most monotonous task in the mill . . . maybe the world. Often equipment would break down during the graveyard shift, and I struggled to stay awake in the sticky night air drifting inland from the nearby harbor. Occasionally the "White Hat" or shift manager would walk by as I nodded off. He was aware of the monotony and kept walking. Bosses carry their own emotional baggage, but the good ones appreciate workers who get the job done without complaining too much.

Confucius is quoted as saying, "If you love your work, you will never work a day in your life." This is an exaggeration. Most of us do not love work that much, but we *can* decide to do our work as an act of service to God and people no matter what the job consists of and no matter what the pay.

Reflection: How will it affect your level of satisfaction at work if you consciously regard work as service to God?

GROWING CHARACTER

Power and Control

Slow Down

Strength

Telling the Truth

Waiting

Wanting

Power and Control

Unresolved issues of power and control kill people. One event illustrated this in a horrifying way. The story is of a man, so angry that his ex-wife had custody of their children, that he killed them and himself in order to take away control from his ex. Power has a voracious appetite, eating everything in its path. We cannot feel what others feel when we are full of our own desperate sense of insignificance. Perhaps twisted insignificance drove a young German to his former job site where he shot two employers before going to his old high school and murdering the principal.

These are examples of desperate attempts to obtain power and control, but we need a certain amount of these two qualities to live. God gave Adam and Eve power as keepers of creation. He gave legitimate power to establish his kingdom on earth. As God's sons and daughters, we were to rule the earth and nurture creation. God does not give us work without power to do it.

The instinct to have control is observable from the time we leave the womb. When one of our children was born, the doctor said it was one of the easiest deliveries he had seen. "Easy for him to say," my wife quipped. The first cries of our baby suggested the precious little one did not think it was such an easy passage either.

At birth, we come out screaming for someone to meet our needs. As we grow into childhood, we may try to gain control over other people, including parents. Unless the instinct to be in control is surrendered to God, it ruins relationships. The desire to control leads to blaming siblings when we are caught doing wrong. As we get a little older, we blame the boss, the company, the pastor, our parents, or even our children for our decisions, unaware that in doing so we are actually giving *them* control of our lives.

We become dangerous when we overstep the legitimate boundary of power and control. That boundary is the belief that God has our best interests at heart, and he will not hold back anything we should have. Here is the first lie Satan told people: God is hiding something from us that we should have. As a result, we may be deceived into suspecting God does not love us. If we do not believe he does, we don't believe we should trust or obey him. Unbelief can lead to either hideous or subtle manipulative attempts to control people and our environments.

But the true value of our lives is not calculated by control over circumstances or people. Instead, we discover value by immersing ourselves in God's grace each day, believing he has love and purpose for us. In loving and obeying him, we break free from addiction to power and control, and we grow into responsible servants who change our world.

Instead of grappling for control, we can be confident that God is weaving our acts of service into an epic story.

Reflection: In what relationship do you struggle with issues of power and control? What first step can you take to resolve this struggle?

Slow Down

Everybody makes mistakes driving, but some people treat the highway like a race track. When somebody imitates Indy and cuts me off in traffic, my brain defaults to autopilot where it repeats sarcastic phrases: "Attaboy. Drive like an idiot!" "Good job, moron!" etc. With God's help, I am reprogramming my inner pilot.

Some things immediately bump my anger button. My default pattern when I face those things is sarcasm, often unspoken. What's your default? Autopilot reactions may worsen situations and drive people away. How can we reprogram our defaults so that powerful feelings do not sideswipe us? Even if we learn the world's best anger management principles, when we face disagreement or roadblocks, we easily ditch principles and maintain the rapid, sometimes angry, pace. Habits and reactions become entrenched through years of repetition.

We can find a better way, but it takes prayer and persistence. These things change the tempo, not of traffic, but of our thinking. For example, we cannot control how someone else drives, but we *can* control *our* driving. More importantly, we can control our reactions to someone else's decisions. An old anecdote says that when we are angry, we should count to ten before speaking. It takes time for the initial geyser of frustration to settle before we can focus on what really matters. Slowing down creates space to ask:

- What's the worst that could happen if I don't get there as quickly as I want to?
- How ugly will this meeting become if I vent my anger carelessly?
- If I take longer to reach this goal, will it make any difference?

It does not matter whether we are trying to "wrap" a video game, get to a meeting early, or complete a manuscript for an editor. Slowing our thinking is a powerful little tool. We can use it when tension or frustration is pushing our ears up to our shoulders or our necks are kinked from anxiety. When the tempo of life makes enjoying good things impossible, slow down.

Reflection: When do you need to allow more time to do something well rather than be frustrated that it's taking too long?

Strength

What makes a person strong? Is it the speedy dexterity of Jackie Chan, wreaking havoc on opponents without breaking a sweat? Is it power to move others with a song, like Pavarotti shaking the rafters or a diva drawing tears from listeners? Are you strong if you have a physique that can lift five hundred pounds overhead in a single motion? Are you macho if you can lift your bride over the threshold of your first home? Despots are able to destroy the well-being of entire ethnic groups by ordering genocide against them. Still others market terror through guerilla warfare or threaten the use of nuclear war. Is that real strength?

As a young man, I spent considerable time trying to develop muscles and speed. Fitness can be addictive. One feels the rush of pushing through a new barrier to faster time or heavier weight. Finishing the race and knowing I had bettered my time and had run faster than before gave me a sense of relief and power. Yet strength has a way of slipping away with years no matter how we fight to preserve it. Some time ago, I spoke at the funeral of a friend who died of cancer. Her vibrant personality is silent, and her strong idealism is no longer with us. What is real strength when facing the reality of human frailty and death?

For one thing, real strength is control of the temper. Israel's King Solomon wrote that someone who controls his temper is stronger than someone who conquers a city (Proverbs 16:31). It takes great strength to take a city. I watched news portraying American troops, under the direction of General Schwartzkopf, entering Kuwait City in the late 1980s. That victory required intense preparation and great expense. Controlling one's temper requires more strength than a mighty military exercise. It takes strength of character.

Real strength is also the ability to control what we say. The apostle James said that if you can keep your words in line, you can keep your whole body in check (James 3:2-5). James goes on to describe the tongue as something evil and even deadly.

Given the power of temper and the tongue, it seems doubtful that anyone could control them. It is possible, however, to overcome through first admitting our weakness and then humbly depending upon the power of God. Through daily surrender to him, we may control temper and hurtful words. *A growing character is quieter than an immature one.*

Mother Teresa of Calcutta was an example of real strength. She appeared, from the surreal distance of television, as a frail, little old woman, yet she captivated the world with few words and countless, potent acts. Others followed in her steps because they could see that she was changing her world. She was a woman of influence who left a legacy of servanthood. While the strength of empires crumble and iron-fisted dictators are forgotten, people honor the memory of Mother Teresa and others who humbly transform their world through real strength.

Reflection: What source of strength have you held in high esteem, and is that source making your world a better place?

Telling the Truth

As a small boy, I looked at the shoes of a woman who was visiting my mother and said, "Your shoes look just like rowboats!" I told the truth as I perceived it; however, the truth was not helpful! Telling the truth consistently in order to be helpful is an adult discipline to be nurtured. In contrast to my childish, albeit childlike, honesty, my grown-up version has acquired the skill of rationalizing my character flaws, overrating my motives, and excusing my bad attitude. After all, my self argues, I spoke sharply because I was tired after a long day! What similar lies might you be telling yourself about your motives, your skills, your character, or your relationships with God and people?

We live in a world where lying is a prime-time feature. Television sitcoms are often built around the trouble caused by a character, either a bumbling husband or a slightly unbalanced woman, trying to cover up the latest lie. We are led to believe that smart people do not get caught, and that "white lies" are harmless. But so-called harmless lies destroy our reputations with the very people whose trust we desire. Why do we tell lies?

- Lying is convenient. Have you ever told someone you are too busy to spend the evening with him when the truth is you would rather stay home alone and watch television?
- Lying prevents truth from hurting your friend's feelings, but lets your friend continue in a dangerous lifestyle.
- Lying protects reputations . . . for a while.
- Lying helps avoid rejection until you can no longer stomach being a phony. Then you tell the truth and face . . . rejection.
- Lying makes one's image look better than it really is—at least in the mirror.

A husband and wife named Ananias and Sapphira were part of the first church in Jerusalem. There was such a strong sense of community in their church that people sold possessions and land in order to support each other's financial need. This couple sold property and presented part of the money to the leaders of the church, implying that the gift included the entire proceeds of the sale. Peter confronted each of them and told them their money had been theirs to do with as they pleased. However, he asked them why they had lied to the Holy Spirit, and before they could answer, they died. The fear of the Lord filled the church at that point. No doubt! To God, the truth is not negotiable. If we begin a pattern of lying, we will need more lies to cover up the previous lies. Since we cannot remember every lie, we will be caught in our own webs of deception.

Liars often begin believing their own lies. Friends and family members eventually lose faith in them, yet they continue weaving fantasies, while others avoid them. As a result, they live in insulated worlds of make-believe where they deceive themselves and a few other unfortunate victims.

So how do we tell the truth? When I was in my teens, I had one of those feel-good posters on my bedroom wall. The poster said, "The greatest truths are the simplest." In other words, truth *is* the simplest form of communication. That's why little children often tell it so clearly. They are uninhibited. When I commented on the woman's shoes, I told the simple truth as I saw it, but my words were not kind or necessary. When the truth must be told, we must tell it with love. When we do this, we grow into more mature, stable grown-ups.

Telling the truth may be lonely at times. Someone may misunderstand or despise you for telling the truth, even if you tell it in the gentlest manner and with the purest motive. Lying, on the other hand, is a complicated and lonely way to live.

Reflection: Are you telling yourself the truth about you, or are you telling yourself what you want to hear?

Waiting

Waiting is good! That statement could start a revolution in a culture where instant is optimal. Several years ago, I went shopping with my daughter. She knew what she wanted to purchase, and we were soon standing in line, waiting to pay. We were in a gigantic warehouse store where you find the item, often in a cardboard box in aisle three hundred or some far-off corner, and then take it to a checkout. The line was long, and the cashier had a problem with a customer's receipt and gift certificate. Eventually, the clerk called a supervisor who took even more time.

The man behind us was obviously frustrated with the delay. First, he muttered in a barely audible voice. His volume grew with his frustration. Soon, he started talking out loud to his wife. I sensed she had to agree or be accused of being the reason they were there in the first place. I thought of telling the guy to find another line, since there were at least a half-dozen to choose from, but his attitude was not my problem. He became more and more agitated. "Ridiculous!" he said. "I hate it when people don't know what they're doin'!" His tirade was continuous. My daughter, who was leaning against me by this time, commented on how long it was taking. I answered her loudly enough that the impatient man could hear me. "It's okay," I said. "I've got nothing but time."

Today I realize how self-righteous my comment was. Maybe the impatient man heard me. In any case, he turned down his rant and fumed more quietly. I thought of suggesting that he move ahead of us. Then again, I wasn't sure if I meant to be gracious or if I just wanted him to feel like an idiot. I shut up and waited. Finally, we reached the young cashier. I left, hoping the next guy would not take out his frustration on her. She was not his problem. His problem was his belief that waiting is offensive. He seemed to believe that he deserved better.

I am afflicted with the same belief. Maybe you are too. Have you yelled at the driver ahead of you in traffic, or muttered under your breath loudly enough to register your displeasure, while standing in line at a store? But waiting is good. If we slow our rapid pace and care for our souls and those around us, we are healthier physically, mentally, and spiritually. In fact, we would more often avoid car accidents and mishaps that complicate or even shorten our lives.

Waiting is good. In fact, waiting is essential to faith and maturity. To wait is to believe that God is in control and that he has purpose in what he does; to wait is an act of faith (Psalm 27:13, 14). So, next time the line is moving too slowly, thank God for a chance to grow.

Reflection: What beliefs do you hold to that make waiting difficult?

Wanting

I found the big, old car in the classifieds. It looked great in the vendor's garage. "Only fifty thousand original miles," the owner said. The old boat was loaded. The huge backseat was so wide the kids could hardly touch each other. Power leather seats, power antenna, power everything made it very comfortable. It was more like an extra room than a car. I could imagine, as I sat behind the wheel, that I had power. The old Mercury glided like a cloud down the highway. The power of the 460-cubic-inch motor could leave the "competition" behind at the slightest push of the gas pedal. Just move out, and let the force press you into the driver's seat. Alas, it had a taste for gasoline, and every time we filled the tank, we added oil in large quantities. As the potential for repair bills began to stack up, I had to decide whether to pour more money into the bad purchase or get rid of it. In the end, I took it to an auction and walked away with the minimum payment. I lost my shirt, but I learned some things about wanting too much.

I have made enough bad purchasing decisions to recognize the power of want. Car commercials know what I like. But because I could not afford the new ones in the commercials, I developed a taste for older models that just needed a little loving attention and the touch of the right tools. The older cars were new to me, though I usually learned why they were too old for someone else.

I am not the only one the commercials target successfully. A study revealed that Canadians on average incomes require over seventy weeks to earn what they spend in fifty-two. What is wrong with this picture? As the saying goes, "You have to learn to want what you have rather than have what you want." Market researchers understand our desire for *more* things, whether we need them or not.

Want is like a disease that controls and corrupts if we do not manage it well. Recently, I was contemplating another car deal. I was tired of my older model. I wanted to upgrade, but lessons from bad decisions and from Scripture intervened, and I avoided the purchase. While cars are for transportation, car commercials are not selling transportation. They sell prestige, power, belonging, less anxiety, and more sex appeal. The pressure to spend on wants can make a consumer miserably dissatisfied. On the other hand, if we buy cars for transportation, clothes for modesty, and food for nutrition, we will enjoy life more. This does not mean that we should not like hot cars, fine clothes, or delicious food, but want takes control if we *must* have things we cannot afford.

Jesus made it clear that important values go deeper than want. He said that even flowers and birds depend upon their heavenly Father to meet their needs (Matthew 6:28-30). Want less. Live more.

Reflection: What do you want so much that you focus your attention on acquiring it? Is it worthwhile?

CELEBRATING FAMILY

❧

Generations

Love

Parents

Sex

Spiritual Heritage

Generations

I think most fathers would confess feeling unprepared to be dads when their children are born or adopted. I remember being wonder-struck at how precious and pure each of our children was when he or she came into the world. But in hindsight, I realize I started this journey of fatherhood with unrealistic expectations. For example, I thought I would be like my dad and my children would be like me. I was not aware of these expectations for many years, but one day, frustrated with myself and my limits as a parent, I saw my illusion for what it was. I am like my dad, but unlike him, and my children are like me, but unlike me. Each is an individual with unique gifts, dreams, and personalities. One generation is different than the next, especially in this quickly changing world. But you should celebrate the diverse personalities, abilities, and experiences of your children. So I say to adult children, "Don't try to be your parents, even if they were successful."

I was slow to learn this, but one day I was "hangin' out" with one of my sons. We went to the football parade, and cheered for our team's float. Later, we shopped at a large downtown mall with more stores than we cared to see, stopping for lunch in a crowded food court. After we had our fill of the mall and its menu, we drove across the city to a discount warehouse where we found early Christmas gift bargains and some cool hardware. Our last stop was a large theater where we chose one of twelve movies that were playing that day. We had a good time. I was able to slow down enough to hear my own heart and my son's words.

As we talked, I reflected out loud that my life as a child and teenager was vastly different from his. There was little time to "hang out" on the farm since there was always work to do. High school football season, for example, fell during harvest time, and it was understood at our house that harvest was a higher priority than football. We did not travel much, and spending a day in a large, downtown mall or attending a parade were not on our radar. But we didn't care because home was a happy, loving place. After listening to me ramble a little about my past and the differences between our respective childhoods, my son looked at me and said nonchalantly, "Don't worry about it, Dad. I like you just the way you are."

When children are born, you feel as though they are tiny extensions of you. They are totally dependent on your love, care, and protection, yet they are individuals whose independence will gradually emerge. They are marvelous new persons with God-given personalities that will be shaped by unique circumstances. Though your influence on them is undeniable, they will grow beyond you.

Parents are a child's early picture of God. Some people reject God because a dad or a mom, even one who professed to know God, was cruel, unpredictable, manipulative, or continually angry. "If God is like this," the subconscious mind asks, "why would I want to have anything to do with him?" So, you are not your parents, and you are not God, but if you celebrate God's love for you, you will have more love left over for your children.

Reflection: In what ways are you similar to and different from your parents?

Love

The simple sign said, "Above all men on earth, I love you, Dad." It was carved into a piece of castaway wood from an old bunk bed frame. I kept this treasured gift from my son's heart. It was a reminder to embrace little opportunities to say "I love you." As children enter teen years, we parents sometimes think they do not want us bothering them with the "mushy stuff." Sometimes this is true, but love helps kids make sense of their ever-changing lives. Not only is this true for teens, but also for children, moms, dads, and everybody else. In fact, the Bible says that, of the big three—faith, hope, and love—love lasts forever.

I was thinking about love as I wrote this because I just re-read a Valentine I wrote to my wife a couple of weeks before. She's really something. In fact, I hope someday each of our kids has a love that is as honest and loyal as she.

Thinking about love made me wonder why I don't pay *more* attention to the ones I love. Is it because my life is too busy? Is it easy to miss the obvious beauty of love when I worry about finances? Love can be tough to remember when the calendar is too full, yet love gives meaning to the days on that calendar. Maybe we neglect love when we do not feel it as strongly as we want to, and so we fear love is lost. This appears to be the reason for many failed marriages and more than a few hit songs that say, explicitly or not, "I don't love you anymore." A growing love is nurtured by countless, little decisions and gestures of kindness. If we neglect love, we often do so because we think it should be a good feeling instead of a good decision. The Bible says we should love one another because love comes from God (1 John 4:7). It does not say, "Let's feel good about each other so that we can be kind to each other."

No. Love consistently chooses the other person's good and makes life livable. Without love, there is no purpose to the schedule. I have walked with many families through the process of planning a funeral for a loved one. Yet, I have never heard a grieving person say, "I wish I had spent less time loving and more effort earning money, getting more degrees, or working overtime." Love and achievement are not mutually exclusive, but they *are* a question of priorities.

So, let us love others, especially family and close friends, with the kind of loyalty we would like to receive. Ironically, we most easily overlook the *most* important people in our lives. Maybe we do this because we assume they will always be there, or because, along with their good points, they have problems that can give us a pain in the neck . . . or the heart. For a dozen years, I watched my dad love my mom through the distance that Alzheimer's Disease creates. She was unable to return the same love he brought during faithful, regular visits to the nursing home.

Real love hurts sometimes because real lovers are ordinary folks with extraordinary weaknesses. That is one reason we need each other so much. For every tough thing about real love, there are a thousand hurts when people give up on love and chase self-centered fantasies. Love takes a lifetime, and eventually all the other stuff we think is important falls away. Why don't we learn a love that seeks the other person's best interests? It is never too late to start, but the longer we leave it, the more unloving habits we have to break. Above all things on earth, an honest love will outlast the decaying power of time. Love sees beauty where others see castaway wood.

Reflection: If you have neglected someone, what will you do to show love to that person?

Parents

As a parent, I have wondered if I could have done more to prevent the event. In hindsight, the "crisis" looks relatively minor, but for those few hours, it loomed large and dark in the night. Silently, I interrogated myself. Should we have moved to another community? Would that have provided a better environment in which to raise our children? Maybe, if we had chosen different education options, things would have been different. I questioned whether I should have left our church and found another community to worship and grow in. Was I even competent enough to raise children in the first place?

Late at night, the questions outnumbered the answers. What parent has not asked questions like these? Fear and doubt have more power when one lays awake in the dark. My imagination inflated my fear into terrible scenarios for the future, compounding the crisis, envisioning disaster.

As I tossed and turned, another voice whispered in my mind, arresting my doubts and fears. God's Spirit spoke a pointed message in my mind. "Give your head a shake," he seemed to say. "The world isn't a perfect place. You can't protect children from reality, but you can and must teach them to confront it with grace and truth. There is *no place* where you can protect them from the real world, but you can trust me. I love your children more than you know." With those calming thoughts, I fell asleep.

That night helped me face an outstanding issue. I wanted to control circumstances, but the quiet voice in the night reminded me I am not in control. At the same time, all of us have choices. As a parent, I chose to be where I am, because I believed God led us here. Furthermore, children have choices. No one can stand before God and blame Mom and Dad. Someday, it will be clear that we have all made our own decisions. In a culture of blame, we assume someone— leaders, parents, society—must be responsible when things go badly for us. At the end of the story, however, we will see that we spoke our own lines while God directed the drama of our lives. We have the tremendous power of choice.

Letting go of our children is one of life's difficult choices, yet it is a necessary step of faith. So, we live with these parallel truths: God is in control, and we have the power of choice. Where these intersect has baffled theologians for thousands of years. What is clear is that we are responsible for choices, and no one shapes our attitudes without our permission. Choices reveal whom we most trust, even in the lonely night.

Reflection: What problem, perceived or real, keeps you awake at night? Is there a legitimate reason why you cannot let it go?

Sex

Sex is like nuclear energy. And, like nuclear energy, sex is wonderful. Doctors rely on nuclear energy for the production of isotopes for cancer treatment. Nuclear power heats homes on cold winter nights with power from nuclear reactors. And power from those same reactors lights up dark evenings. Nuclear energy provides jobs and contributes to the economy. It is a healing, productive power. Yet that same energy, when it escapes the confines designed to keep it safe and productive, corrupts crops and poisons people as it did when the Chernobyl reactors melted down. And nuclear power destroys entire cities when bombs explode in the atmosphere. In other words, this power can be devastating, vaporizing entire communities.

Like nuclear power, sex is a wonderful gift that builds families and heals the soul when lovers express their sexuality together. However, sex can also destroy families, corrupt neighborhoods, and destroy society. What decides whether sex is healing or deadly? Just as scientists developed nuclear energy for use in a safe, healthy environment, God created sex for a committed, exclusive marriage covenant between one man and one woman. To say God is cruel for insisting this gift be kept to marriage is like saying science is mean for keeping nuclear power in reactors. Or, to say one does not believe sex is beautiful just because one preserves sex for marriage is like saying one rejects nuclear medicine just because one says nuclear warheads are destructive. Same substance, different applications.

If one were to build a building without ensuring the foundation is square, one would eventually tear down the building because he did not begin right. Similarly, relationships that begin with unreserved passion instead of growing friendship more easily dissolve when upheaval shakes the relationship.

Some argue that sex should be explored before marriage—that one cannot be sure "it will work" unless they have a sexual relationship before marriage. However, I have observed that couples who decide that waiting for sex is foolish face more instability than those who wait. There are exceptions to this, but not many. The plain truth is that if both partners commit to making life good for each other, their sexual relationship will be enriched. On the other hand, if they will not commit to loving each other no matter what, sex will not save their relationship.

Reflection: What common attitudes toward sex do you hear in your conversations with your peers?

Spiritual Heritage

As we celebrated another one of Dad's ninety-something birthdays, I thought about the spiritual heritage my parents and their parents before them handed down to me. A spiritual heritage is more than a sense of history and roots. History is important, but spiritual heritage is a deeper, broader footing—a foundation for values and decisions. Yet as profound an impact as one's heritage might have, it only takes one generation to discard the faith nurtured and entrusted to us by those who have gone before.

However, we must not keep faith merely because, like an heirloom, it is in the family. You do not inherit faith; you choose it. At a point in time, I decided to ask Jesus to come into my life. That day, I became his. It took more than information or family tradition to convince me I needed him. I needed convincing that only God could give. So it is for every person in every generation. Parents and other family members have a profound influence, demonstrating by the way they live that faith is real. They give the next generation an engaging, inviting diary of the living Christ, capable of influencing life choices. But each generation chooses faith for itself.

As a young man, my grandfather came to faith when he heard a preacher explain who Jesus is and what he has done for us. Both my parents committed their lives to him in their teen years, and they continued to trust him when hard times and poverty could have driven them to abandon faith and search for an easier way. Instead, they leaned more heavily on God. Everyone chooses whether to persevere in faith or quit. We have many opportunities to trust him in daily choices. Which college will we attend? Where will we live? What career will we choose? Will we confront our weaknesses? Will we sacrifice our time to help a friend through trouble?

Daily decisions concerning character and faith have a powerful impact. Will we live in our beliefs when we could emigrate to a more popular trend or to the values of our peers? Will we take opportunities to use our gifts well or sit on the sidelines, letting others carry the responsibility? Will we serve people well when we are already tired, or will we leave the work to someone else? These decisions sustain or decay a heritage. If we let the tide of circumstance, social pressure, and peer pressure sweep away our faith, a new generation flounders in unbelief and lost opportunities, failing to move forward in faith and impact still another generation. Either way, it only takes one generation.

Reflection: From today forward, are you going to strengthen or weaken the spiritual foundation for your family?

Building Healthy Relationships

Being in Love

Conflict

Disagreements

Forgiveness

Friends

Being in Love

I am convinced many marriages are unhappy or broken because men expect their brides to be goddesses but wake up the next morning to a mere woman—the same woman day after day. Similarly, women expect their grooms to be gods but find out they are not very good listeners and pathetic at answering prayer. Over time, marriage partners' expectations are repeatedly dashed on the rocks of reality. She doesn't always understand his dreams; a goddess would, and she would devote her life to helping him become everything he imagines he can be. On the other hand, he doesn't always pay attention to the little things that make a big difference to her; a god would know just when she needs a hug, a gentle word of encouragement, or a decisive act. As a result, one or both partners get stuck in a childish fantasy and begin looking elsewhere to gratify the myth of the perfect partner—perhaps the cute barista or the guy at work who listens. The search is never truly satisfied because men and women cannot meet each others' deepest longings for love and acceptance. They are merely people, and people fail. So if you are disappointed in your partner, try walking on water; if you cannot, chances are you are not worthy of marriage to a god or goddess anyway!

When barely a teenager, I told God I was in love with a girl and asked him to work things out for me. Sometimes, I thank God he does not answer my prayers in the way I would like him to. How do we know we are in love? Is it when we can't forget that guy or girl we just met? Does true love happen when we see a face or physique that stands out?

We should also ask, "Do I *need* this relationship in order to feel worthwhile?" If we answer, "Yes," we must realize that we need to experience God's love in order to love well. Even a prettier, stronger human being is unable to fulfill the need for wholeness. On the other hand, if that new, beautiful person moving into a single person's heart can accept yet kindly confront weaknesses, this might be real love. If one accepts another's weaknesses yet celebrates his or her strengths, one is learning love. Being in love does not mean we are blind to every other beauty in the world or that we suddenly find every *other* member of the opposite sex unattractive. It means we care enough about someone to commit to an exclusive love.

We know we are in love when we save sexual intimacy for marriage instead of pressing a partner to go to bed. In other words, the relationship is not based on sex but respect and understanding. Such a foundation underlies better sex in marriage. Many people think they have to live with a partner before marriage in order to find out if they are compatible. I am not sure if this is an excuse to get between the sheets or sincere confusion about what makes relationships last. If one loves and respects his partner, the sex will be great.

We know we are in love when we are just a little afraid to commit to each other because we consider the marriage covenant such a sacred bond. Then we know we need God's help to make it last. A wiser, older friend counseled me as I wrestled with fear of failing the person I loved, though I wanted to spend the rest of my life with her. He bluntly asked, "Can you be everything she needs you to be as her husband?" I started to nod "Yes," but he answered the question for me. "No, you can't!" he said. "You're going to have to depend on God to help you." At the time, I felt his words like one feels a smack to the skull, but his advice was right and worth passing along.

We know we are in love when we are willing to grow up enough to learn that love is more than a feeling. Another older, wiser man listened to my fear of commitment. What if I could see her imperfections—her basic humanness? Was this a sign I did not really love her? He wrote a number on a piece of paper. I think he wrote "Ninety percent." Then he asked if I liked that much about her, and if I did, that was an extremely high mark. Again, I nodded.

Sometimes perfectionism stifles love. Perhaps we are afraid of reality. Fantasy is easier to live with, as long as we do not mind being alone. Do we see love as a beautiful ride through a theme park or an endless carefree stroll along a warm, sandy beach? Life is not like that, and neither is love. No matter how much one loves a spouse, he or she might have a trait or habit that drives one nuts! But we learn to laugh and accept the annoying traits along with the great ones. Those perfect, model partners we might fantasize about only exist on a poster or in a magazine.

We know we are in love when we are able to accept the truth that God enjoys giving gifts like wonderful relationships. I was in love, but wondered if something was going to go wrong, either in my own heart or in the relationship. I was struggling under the illusion that God could not want me to spend my life devoted to loving someone I was enchanted by. Could he really be that good—that interested in my life? Somehow, I conveyed my worries to my mother in a phone conversation. Though she rarely gave advice when I was a young adult, she sent a letter reminding me that God gives good things. After pointing out that God did indeed love me, she quoted Psalm 16:11 and pointed out that he plans to give joy to his people.

God gives love for us to hold with firm care and nurture with humble confidence. He wants the best for us. As parents dream of healthy, happy futures for their children, the heavenly Father dreams of wholeness for you and me. We know we are in love when we are firmly in his embrace and, therefore, able to hold firmly to someone else. Every marriage has some undercurrents that could pull it down; the key is to learn to swim together with the power of God's love.

Reflection: Which of the above statements that define being in love do you find most helpful? Why?

Conflict

Someone said, "It's more important to be kind than to be right." I disagree with that at face value. Without truth, there is no kindness—only sentiment. A better phrase would be, "It's *just as* important to be kind as right."

The New Testament lays the foundation for this idea when it says we become mature as we speak the truth in love (Ephesians 4:15). If we tell the truth *without* love, we alienate those we are trying to convince. Since we cannot always avoid conflict and still maintain integrity, the question is whether we must win every battle. We are not boxers who enter the ring with the goal of beating our opponents.

Sometimes we assume people are looking for trouble when they are not. Other times, conflict aims at us as though our foreheads have bull's-eyes painted on them. Conflict can appear suddenly, like a good, quick jab, leaving us dazed and wondering why we did not see it coming.

Here are some principles for managing conflict instead of crushing opponents:

- If you cannot honestly talk to God about a conflict you will have a tough time resolving it. He will help you deal with your attitude. For example, when another driver flips you the bird or acts threateningly, say, "God, you know what that driver needs. Please teach him whatever you want him to know. I can't carry his problem."

- Read the Bible for wisdom in conflicts. For example, in the book of Proverbs, you will find wisdom, and in the Gospels, you will find Jesus' timeless example.

- Expect conflict. Why should you be exempt from it? No on else is.

- Listen first. Understand what people want. Conflict occurs when two or more people have different expectations of the same experience. Try to find out what the other person wants and feels beneath his frustration.

- Be assertive about what you want without being aggressive. Calmly repeating what you want is not offensive to *most* people. Gentle words help diffuse anger.

- Count the cost. If you can avoid costly battles without losing integrity, do so.

- Do everything in your power to treat people as you would like to be treated. Your respect communicates to others that you value them as persons.

- Act with integrity even when others question your motives. Someday, most people will see your character for what it is.

- Pick battles with care. Few hills are worth dying for.
- Learn from people you conflict with. Their perspective could help you grow.
- Pray for them . . . again and again. As God answers your prayers for others, he will change your heart too.

These principles for managing conflict are useful in heart-pounding attacks or friendly debates. God will not leave us alone in either place. Conflict is inevitable; kindness is a choice.

Reflection: What current conflict should you apply one or more of these principles to?

Disagreements

Sometimes people will say things you find far-fetched. You might even think their arguments are stupid and feel that your role is to help them smarten up. But if you must disagree, disagree well. After all, people are sensitive about their ideas. You do not have to say, "That's a dumb idea," to offend someone. You may offend others simply by ignoring them, answering with a tone that says, "I'm smarter than you," or interrupting their suggestions by rolling your eyes or laughing quietly.

I recall a planning meeting during which I suggested a new approach to a recurring problem. The leader said, "No, we're not doing that." There ended the discussion. My idea might not have worked, but I would have learned more had we explored its strengths and weaknesses. I remember another meeting where I quickly scuttled someone else's idea. Not only was I unfair, but I sank the idea before it left the dock.

Although you cannot always agree with others, even those you love, you can disagree agreeably. And if you disagree respectfully, you have a better-than-fifty-percent chance of strengthening the relationship. Conversely, if two people never disagree, one of them is not thinking. Friends who always see things your way or agree just to make you feel good about yourself are not your best friends. Instead, they mislead you to believe you are always right.

So, what is healthy disagreement? This is not the same as ridicule that aims to make one look better than the other guy. Instead, you disagree well when you suppress the impulse to defend your territory against an idea that differs from yours. Fear of another's idea often indicates fear that you are losing control. If you obey this fear and fail to explore new things, you lose opportunities to grow and build stronger friendships. Few ideas are evil or destructive. When they are, you should take a stand. However, most disagreements are not matters of life or death. Here are two suggestions for healthy disagreement:

- Ask for more information. Be sure you understand, as well as you are able, what the other person thinks and why. You will find others less defensive and more open to your ideas if you treat theirs with respect.
- If you happen to disagree, say, "I see things a bit differently." Then explain your perspective. By saying this, you communicate insight instead of condemnation. Then you can discuss things in a mature manner and arrive more quickly at an understanding or consensus.

If you handle disagreement respectfully, there is no guarantee others will do the same. Sometimes you will work with someone whose self-image is so small that he feels your ideas are a threat. Most people, however, respond in kind to the respect they receive. When you must disagree, and you sometimes must, do so well.

Reflection: With whom do you disagree? What can you do to make the disagreement healthy?

Forgiveness

I thought I should try to rebuild a friendship, so I told a friend that he had offended me. He answered, "If you're looking for an apology, you're wasting your time." Forgiveness is more difficult when the other person does not value the relationship, and the relationship often does not recover. But forgiving someone who hurt you takes away his power over you; you stop expecting him to be more than he is or perhaps more than he can be. Furthermore, forgiving makes it possible to appreciate another person for who he is instead of resenting him for what he is not. Ultimately, however, forgiveness is giving grace in much the same way God gives grace to us.

Moreover, forgiveness is a daily diet for a healthy soul. In other words, you do not live long before you need to forgive someone. For example, Jesus' friend Peter asked how many times he should forgive an offender. Peter then suggested seven times as a reasonable number, but Jesus countered that Peter should forgive an offense seventy times seven

(Matthew 18:21, 22). Imagine a stunned Peter, pondering that! Yet, 490 times is not the limit of forgiveness; Jesus' point was that forgiveness is continual. I think Peter needed to forgive someone or longed for forgiveness and a new beginning. Maybe he had lied, failed to be loyal to a friend, or neglected a duty. We know he could turn on his closest friend because, when Jesus was arrested and put on trial, Peter denied ever knowing him.

Conversely, Jesus modeled forgiveness of people who expressed no sorrow for their deeds. Right from the cross, he prayed that God would forgive those who were killing him (Luke 23:34). In praying this, Jesus revealed this truth about some offenses: People are not always aware of the serious harm they do each other. For example, they might offend others without being aware they have done so. As a consequence of humanity's spiritual and social blindness, Jesus demonstrated forgiving as an act of grace, acknowledging the limitations of those he forgave.

But there are times when we are the perpetrators of hurt, not the recipients. In those instances, we might be tempted to justify ourselves with the belief that the other person deserves our wrath. Yet, we are not equipped to judge others' motives. In summary, forgiveness and reconciliation are difficult, but whether we are hurt or guilty of hurting someone, these principles are worth remembering:

- Forgiveness is something we do with God's help. When we ask God for his grace and believe he gives freely, we have grace to give away.

- Reconciliation cannot grow deeper than our will to trust. Trust is limited by the maturity and character of both parties in the relationship.
- Boundaries, which do not allow others to "own" us, are essential. In vibrant relationships, individuals think for themselves.
- Close friends and family need forgiveness. No one was closer to Jesus than Peter and the brothers James and John, yet they sometimes made ridiculous statements. He corrected their ignorance, called them friends, and told them he loved them.
- Forgiveness does not equal agreement. It means we care enough to persevere when love takes extra work.
- No on loves perfectly. Therefore, forgiveness is an essential life skill.
- Everybody needs forgiveness sometime.
- God loves us all the same—the offender and the offended.
- God's grace is greater than any wrong.

When I asked for forgiveness, God forgave me and left my sin in the past, forgotten, washed away. Moreover, he erased it from my record. This is the message known as the gospel—the good news. Since I receive God's train-load of grace, I ought to offer it to others. As a case in point, the apostle Paul reflected on his old sources of significance—heritage, status, religious zeal—and said that compared to knowing Christ, those things were worthless. In other words, many of the things others try to take away when they offend us are not worth clinging to anyway. Harboring grudges might prop up our tottery fences of significance—things we believe we need for our worth—but they are worthless compared to knowing Christ.

Reflection: Which principle of forgiveness helps you forgive when doing so is not easy?

Friends

A sports personality defended himself against ridicule from a colleague by saying he was not in business to make friends. He explained that, as we get older, all we have left are our families and a few close friends, and then life ends. I think his depressing statement was a reaction in the heat of the moment. He was disappointed in his colleague's accusation. I also believe he was mistaken. Though it is true you can be hurt in relationships and cynical about people after friends reject you, you need friends.

I have had friends who told me they appreciated me, even loved me, but then decided I was not worth their time. For instance, I regarded an individual as a close friend until I pressed a point of view he disagreed with. He chose not to trust me, and walked out of my life. The lesson? If you believe anything fervently, you may at some point lose a friend. Grieve the loss, but let your friend go. Friends are not so important that you should give up integrity to please them. Some friends stay for a short span of your journey through life. Some last a long way. Few will go the distance. Few should.

Do not let bitterness over a lost friendship darken a corner of your heart. When you feel like cursing a lost friend, do not allow your mind to go there. Commit him to God again—as often as necessary. Years after a friend rejected me, I was driving somewhere when, for some reason, I remembered his accusations. I felt anger as though he had blasted me that very day, and when my cell phone did not work, I roared my disapproval at the phone. Of course, the phone was not the problem. I needed to deal with the memory again.

So, the lesson is not that you should expect to have few friends, but that you should be willing to lose those who do not like you when you follow your convictions. In other words, love people, and free them to go their own way. As a result of adopting a loving, freeing attitude, you will have more and more friends, not fewer. God will probably not tell you to die a lonely old person.

But the question remains: "How many close friendships can you maintain without being absorbed by them?" By way of illustration, even Jesus did not have many close friends. Yet, if anyone had a capacity for friendship, he did, so you would expect him to have a large circle of buddies. Instead, he invested more time with Peter, James, and John than his other friends, and he was closer to John than Peter or James. Although Jesus loved all his friends, he did not let them define his mission. Had he adopted their agenda for his life, he would have avoided the cross and started a political revolution, which served his friends' ambitions and positioned them near his throne. Instead, Jesus endured the cross and, three days later, rose from death to give eternal life to all who trust him to open the door to his eternal kingdom.

So, how many friends are enough? When you have too many "soul mates" you become dependent on what they think of you. And when others' ideas, opinions, and desires control your thoughts, you forget who you are and what you believe. As a result, you become a shallow friend, easy to be with, but easy to do without. Somewhere, there is a balance between loneliness and friendship overdose. A little loneliness helps you value friends more and makes you more accepting of those who do not fit your idea of the perfect friend.

If friends cannot define your life, what *can* you expect from quality friendships? Primarily, good friends respect each other. Therefore, if given the choice, take respect over affection. For instance, friends who like you as long as you agree with their biases will use you but they will not love you. Real friends respect you enough to allow different points of view without smothering your freedom to think. They may disagree, yet still love you.

Furthermore, real friends will respect you enough to let you make choices they would not make, yet they love you enough to tell you if they believe you are going to harm yourself or others. By contrast, people who shower you with affectionate words or vows of loyalty early in a friendship mislead themselves. Do not let them deceive you. They have not fought with you, for you, or beside you. They imagine themselves heroes, but they have paid no price for that status.

In brief, to keep close friends, respect them as you would like them to respect you. What's more, enjoy having casual friends too. Despite the fact that you do not often socialize with them, and perhaps seldom see them, casual friends will encourage you as you encourage them. For this purpose, I believe God arranges "chance encounters" with casual friends. So, cultivate a small number of close friendships and enjoy many other good friends and acquaintances. Be available to help and encourage without expecting every friendship to grow deep. *No one* has a root system deep enough to sustain branches for *everyone* to sit on.

Reflection: Who are your close friends? Who are your casual friends? Are you willing to accept the fact that friends may shift from casual to close and vice versa?

CREATING COMMUNITY

Funerals

People

"Sorry"

Weddings

Words

Funerals

No matter how often I offer pastoral care to grieving people, I am struck by the mystery of life and death. One day you interact with a friend, and the next day you hear of your friend's death. Only the physical part remains as you remember the spirit that animated him or her. You should attend funerals of people you knew well, people you worked with, or close neighbors when you are able to do so. One of the reasons you go to funerals or memorial services is that life is precious; you acknowledge life as a great gift when you acknowledge another's death.

Life is a vapor, and then it is gone. Eulogies, that element of the funeral service when family and friends summarize their loved one's life, always surprise me. I am amazed that a long life, filled with dreams and achievements, can be summed up in a matter of minutes. At funerals, life feels brief; the "file" of one's achievements looks thin. An entire tribute might last one minute of speaking per decade of living. In other words, the brevity of funerals puts life in perspective for those who take themselves too seriously. So memorials and funerals ought to prompt you to see the simple goodness of being alive.

Another conclusion I have reached after participating in many funerals is that only faith makes sense of grief. When deceased loved ones neglected faith, their families pay them tribute as they should, and honor their memory. Yet, surviving family members grieve without the comfort and certain hope cherished by families of those who held to personal faith in God.

Those grieving the loss of someone with convinced, devoted faith in the death and resurrection of Jesus Christ grieve differently. They still grieve, of course, sometimes with great pain. But they have confidence because, by faith, they share in the resurrection of Christ.

Grief contrasts so sharply with pleasure that it makes the latter appear shallow. Mourning, on the other hand, makes you think. When you mourn, you ask deeper questions that challenge you to reconsider your purpose. As a result, you grow a little wiser. In a society where consumerism drives many decisions, the funeral service reexamines your values and prompts you to live from a deeper place.

Reflection: What is it about funerals that make you uncomfortable?

People

People make good friends but lousy gods. A friend once said, "Everybody has an agenda." True enough. And those who tell you they have no agenda usually have the biggest one. "Never be surprised when people act like people," another friend once told me. I have often needed his advice.

Annoying people are tiresome, and they are everywhere: at school, at work, at church, at home, and in the mirror. To get along with people, you have to admit you are among them, made of the same stuff. How on Earth, since Earth is where you have to get along with others, can you sustain relationships with so many annoying people? With billions of people in the world, how can you be healthy when people annoy you? I am exaggerating, but most of us feel fed up with people at one time or another. Two ordinary factors make an extraordinary difference in relationships: Responsibility + Respect = Healthy Relationships

Two word pictures in the wisdom of Solomon illustrate responsibility. First, you might as well have a toothache or a crippled foot as rely on unfaithful people when you are in trouble (Proverbs 25:19). I can identify with the bad tooth. Being a dental coward, I avoid dentists. Don't misunderstand me. Dentists are usually nice people, but drills and metal picks are not my favorite instruments of healing. I successfully avoided visiting the dentist for ten years. As a result, the pain of eating and drinking anything a few degrees different than body temperature burned like an electric fire in my mouth. A painful cavity makes teeth unreliable at meal time.

Similarly, people who are not dependable can hurt you. Try not to become one of them. Being dependable does not mean saying "yes" to every request others have of your time. If you do, you will eventually resent your commitments. However, when you make a commitment, keep it! If you must miss an appointment, call and give a good reason. That's being responsible.

Respect is a close cousin of responsibility and equally necessary if you are to get along with others. Most people respond to respect with respect. But if, for example, you are consistently late for appointments, you communicate disrespect. Others have planned their schedules around the meeting. Why should they wait until you decide to get there? Other examples of disrespect include picking at another person's weaknesses and booing other national anthems. In contrast, respect implies accepting others' strengths *and* weaknesses. It means giving them a fair shot at expressing their points of view. Fair play is essential to healthy relationships.

However, we live in a world where respect is in short supply. For example, media rarely features respectful interaction between political leaders. Character attacks make better sound bytes. If you show respect and act responsibly, you might sometimes feel you are in the minority, but you are not alone.

Still, you will need courage to show respect. So, stop believing other people will not fail you; stop believing you should not be subject to the trouble the rest of the world must face. Your parents failed you? Welcome to humanity. Your church failed you? Welcome to fellowship with real people. The failure of fellow believers may be the most painful, next to the failure of family. Denying your hurt will cripple your spiritual and emotional health, but so will blaming someone else for your failed relationships.

If you are unhappy with your life and you want someone to blame, follow these instructions. First, step into your bathroom. Second, turn on the light. Third, stare into the mirror. Fourth, tell that person that, from now on, he or she is responsible for your lot in life and how you respond to it. Fifth, forgive the person in the mirror for failing to fulfill all your dreams. Finally, thank God for the reflection staring back at you, and ask for his saving grace and power to live with hope and joy instead of blame. Grow up. Stop blaming the world for your troubles. Start living on purpose.

Reflection: What do you need to say to the person in the mirror?

"Sorry"

We used to read our children a story in which a teddy bear learned "magic words." The words were *please, thank you, I'm sorry,* and *excuse me.* These little words have power. They give dignity and respect to family, friends, and even enemies. I am still learning how to use the magic words, particularly "I'm sorry." And there are two things I am learning *not* to say.

First, I'm learning not to say "I'm sorry *if* I hurt you." The word "if" denies responsibility and suggests that the person we hurt is oversensitive. The reason we say, "I'm sorry *if* I hurt you" is because we do not want to acknowledge we have been guilty of causing pain. So we provide a limp, guilt-free apology, hoping it will make the offended person feel better while we avoid responsibility.

For the offended person, this sweeps the offense under the rug rather than bringing healing. Someone confronted me with this one day after I had said, "I'm sorry *if* I hurt you," and pointed out that I had not acknowledged her pain was real. "If" is a small word with great power. Instead say,

"I'm sorry *that* I hurt you." "That" owns the offense and will more likely help the offended person recover and heal the relationship.

Rudyard Kipling knew this when he wrote his famous poem, *If.* The world turns on the word "if." *If* I work, I get paid. *If* I eat too much, I get sick. *If* I govern well, there will likely be peace. *If* I make good choices, my life will bless other people. *If* I steal, I am a thief. *If* I hurt you, I will repent. "If" is a pivotal word for responsibility, so when we use it to condition apologies, we make them vague and insincere. Honesty nurtures friendships. Failure to own what we have done makes them shrivel. Relationships heal, not with "if," but with humble confession.

The other thing I am learning not to say is, "I'm sorry, *but* you weren't fair either." As someone in a conflict once said, "I'm sorry I hurt you, *but* I had to . . . " In others words, *my* wrongdoing is really *your* fault after all. *You* deserve to be hurt! When we say, "I'm sorry but . . . ," we are not sorry at all. Rather, we are blaming the offended person for our decisions.

A sincere apology comes from a heart humble enough to take responsibility for words and actions. In fact, an apology dependent on "if" or "but" gives responsibility and, therefore, power to the other person. "Ifs" and "buts" say my decisions arise from others' actions rather than my will. This is something to keep in mind the next time we need to apologize and we are tempted to say "I'm sorry if . . ." or "I'm sorry, but . . ."

Reflection: When was the last time you said, "I'm sorry," and how was your apology received?

Weddings

My favorite wedding was the one where I left with the bride! The day mattered not because of the flowers, guest list, photos, or food, but because I knew this woman was the one I did not want to live without. What an enormous decision one makes when choosing to marry! What a risk she took tying her life to mine. Once your bride starts down the aisle, your destiny walks with her. That is one of those moments when your life changes before your eyes, when you feel the power of dreams coming true. Weddings bring to the surface some of the deepest truths about love.

Every wedding where the bride and groom create a lasting covenant is special. Some ceremonies exemplify the beginning we would want for our children's marriages. The bride and the groom are committed to following Christ *together*. Their ceremony is a worship experience. The couple—not planning and preparation—is what matters.

I have been at weddings with little planning and many mistakes, but obvious joy. If you have a choice, however, go with the planned version! A plan makes handling the unexpected much easier, and the unexpected is a variable as the wedding day draws near.

A wedding is a community event. So what if you are not invited to the reception? Go to the ceremony! The ceremony is a glimpse of covenant love. Unfortunately, the big dinner and program may dominate the spotlight, and the ceremony is a mere hurdle en route to great food. The more important fact is that family and friends at the wedding have a responsibility to pray for, encourage, and welcome the newly married couple.

Earlier I said that the most important part of a wedding is the couple, but that is not quite true. The most important person at the wedding is God himself. He is not a guest, but the Wonderful Counselor, the Prince of Peace, the Everlasting Father. He is the one who makes life together enjoyable and enduring.

A wedding is as enduring as the love covenant made at the altar. If the relationship has no spiritual dimension, both partners miss the greatest part of their union. A love that stands the tests of time is built on honest communication and vulnerable trust. Both partners have to give one hundred percent for a relationship to be a marriage. I wish you a wonderful marriage. May it be blessed by the presence of God, many faithful, supportive friends, and extra wedding gifts to return for a refund!

Reflection: Of all the weddings you have witnessed, which one did you enjoy the most? What made it enjoyable?

Words

When the movie *Gone with the Wind* appeared, Rhett Butler's language was cavalier. Rough men would curb crude language in the company of ladies. How times change. Now, women in some work contexts freely curse as fluently as men. So how do we evaluate language? Can we set boundaries without creating irrelevant rules? The language question surfaced when a friend asked what I thought about slang and words that some see as bad language. Is it okay, for example, to make the word *crap* a normal part of daily dialogue? And other words, which were once taboo, have become the norm.

Language is a symbol of something deeper, for the mouth speaks from the heart's overflow. This is true of slang as well as angry or slanderous words. What we repress eventually spews out, often with intensity. For example, I felt growing frustration over a couple of work-related issues. Then one evening, one of our children said something that punctured my frustration, and I peppered him with angry words. Later, I apologized for my outburst. Had I first spilled my guts to God, I could have avoided hurting someone I love. Had I sought advice from a friend, I would have gained perspective on my turmoil. Watch over your heart; for it regulates your mouth.

Speech not only reveals our state of mind, it influences what we become. I have a friend who consistently answers "Wonderful!" when others ask how he is. His character and state of mind reflect that attitude. On the other hand, I have noticed that, when I grumble, I create a negative attitude. The point is not that we should fake well-being; the point is that words actually influence how we feel and live. If we speak negatively, we cultivate a sour attitude, but if say we are wonderful, we likely develop a healthier outlook on life.

Crude talk benefits no one. While we might feel temporary relief when spewing coarse language, careless language tears others down. Slang opens the door to coarse language. Actually, the state of the heart can be the same whether we habitually say "crap" or a different four-letter word. Once the lip gate opens, the whole language herd can ride through. Better to be quiet when angry; I have learned that the first words that come to mind when I am angry are better steered away from my tongue and swallowed. Later, after I have asked God for help and maybe talked to a peer or mentor, I can say the right words instead of regrettable ones. Moreover, God can take it when I tell him how angry I feel. And when my words get away from me, he can forgive and forget when I acknowledge my sin. I remember the first time I let my anger pour out in a prayer. Stunned at my own words, I think I expected to feel condemnation. But then I realized that God already knew my mind before it escaped through my mouth. "Let's talk," I think he was saying.

If we guard our hearts and thoughts with prayer, and if we concentrate on the truly good things in life, our speech will be more wholesome. What we feed the mind flows through the mouth. To make my words count, I sometimes ask myself, "If everyone had my standard for language, would the world be a more encouraging place?"

Reflection: What words do you want to add to or delete from your vocabulary?

ABOUT THE AUTHOR

Grant McDowell has been a pastor for thirty-one years. He and his wife Donna have three adult children and a son-in-law whom they enjoy as friends. They live in Leduc, Alberta, Canada, where he has been privileged to serve a local church for twenty-five years. From his interactions with people in various work and social contexts, Grant has come to believe that everyone is in "the people business," and that mentoring is an essential part of everyone's journey through life. He has been recognized in his community with the Mayor's Special Award as a Citizen of Distinction, and he has been honored as Citizen of the Year by the Leduc Regional Chamber of Commerce. Through Gordon-Conwell Theological Seminary, he earned a Doctor of Ministry degree. He is the author of a score of magazine articles in publications including *Leadership*, *Church Executive*, *Business.life*, and others. He contributes a column to the *Leduc Representative* newspaper.

CPSIA information can be obtained at www.ICGtesting.com
Printed in the USA
LVOW10s0422030714

392568LV00003B/12/P